Painting

Sue Stocks

With photographs by Chris Fairclough

Wayland

FIRST ARTS & CRAFTS

This series of books aims to introduce children to as wide a range of media approaches, techniques and equipment as possible, and to extend these experiences into ideas for further development. The National Curriculum proposals for art at Key Stage One place particular emphasis on the appreciation of art in a variety of styles from different cultures and times throughout history. The series broadly covers the National Curriculum attainment targets
1) Investigating and Making and 2) Knowledge and Understanding, but recognizes that circumstances and facilities can vary hugely. Children should experiment with, and add to, all the ideas in these books, working from imagination and observation. They should also work with others, where possible, in groups and as a class. You will find suggestions for and comments about each section of work in the Notes for parents/teachers at the end of the book. They are by no means prescriptive and can be added to and adapted. Unless a particular type of paint or glue is specified, any type can be used. Above all, the most important thing is that children enjoy art in every sense of the word.
Have fun!

Titles in this series
Collage, Drawing, Masks, Models, Painting, Printing, Puppets, Toys and Games

First published in 1994
by Wayland (Publishers) Ltd, 61 Western Road, Hove
East Sussex BN3 1JD, England
© Copyright 1994 Wayland (Publishers) Ltd
Series planned and produced by The Square Book Company

British Library Cataloguing in Publication Data
Stocks, Sue
Painting - (First Arts & Crafts Series)
751.4
ISBN 0 7502 1009 5

Photographs by Chris Fairclough
Designed by Howland ■ Northover
Edited by Katrina Maitland Smith
Printed and bound in Italy by G. Canale & C.S.p.A., Turin

Contents

Looking at colours

What is your favourite colour? Collect ten things that are this colour. Put them together on a table and look at all the different shades.

Go outside and look at the colours. The sky, rooftops, trees, cars, people and flowers are all different colours. Will all the colours you see around you be the same at other times of the year? What colour is the sky on a sunny day? What colour is it on a stormy or a snowy day?

Collect some leaves and look at the different greens, reds, oranges and browns.

4

Artists use different colours to make their paintings.

Look at these two paintings. The top one is *Tours: Sunset*, painted by J. M. W. Turner, an English artist who lived about 150 years ago. The other is *Impression, Sunrise* by Claude Monet, a French artist who lived about 100 years ago.

Their paintings are about the sun. One is a sunrise and the other is a sunset. Have you ever seen skies like these?

What colours would you use to paint a rainy day?

Brushes and techniques

You have seen how colour can create different effects in a painting. You can also create interesting effects using different paints, brushes and other painting tools.

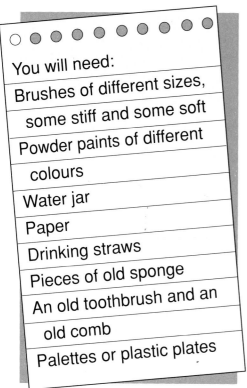

You will need:

Brushes of different sizes, some stiff and some soft

Powder paints of different colours

Water jar

Paper

Drinking straws

Pieces of old sponge

An old toothbrush and an old comb

Palettes or plastic plates

- Mix your paints into two lots. Make one quite thick by mixing the paint with just a little water, and one thinner by adding more water.

- Take a small, soft brush and try painting some straight and wavy lines on the paper with the thick paint. When you press down the line is wide. Paint a narrow line.

- Take a wide, soft brush and the thinner paint. Paint wide strokes across the paper. This is called a wash. Try this brush with the thicker paint. Paint shorter strokes. Criss-cross them to make a pattern.

Experiment by painting lines
and washes with all the brushes
and both the paints. Now try
some other painting tools.

- Dip a stiff brush in the paint.
  Dab the tip of the bristles up
  and down on the paper.

- Dip a piece of sponge into the
  thinner paint. Dab the paint on
  to the paper using the sponge.
  Now try another piece of
  sponge with the thicker paint.

- Dip the head of the toothbrush
  into the thinner paint and use
  the old comb to pull back the
  bristles. Allow the paint to
  spatter over the paper.
- Make a pool of thinner paint in
  the middle of the paper. Hold a
  straw about 3 cm above it and
  blow hard. Keep blowing,
  following the lines of paint.

Colour mixing

You can mix coloured paints together to make other colours.
You can make many different colours with just red, yellow and
blue paints.

You will need:
Brushes
Water jar
Red, blue and yellow
 paints
Paper
Palettes or plastic plates

- Mix red and yellow together. What colour have you made?
- Mix red and blue together. Now what colour have you made?

Try experimenting with different colours to see what you get.

Now take your yellow and red paints.

Paint a yellow square. Add a tiny amount of red to the yellow on your palette and paint your new colour next to the yellow square. Add a little more red and paint another square.

Keep on doing this until the last square you paint is nearly all red. Look at the different shades.

Try again with red and blue, then blue and yellow. Count how many shades you have made from just three colours. Try to think up names for all your colours, like 'tomato red' or 'grass green'.

You can make nearly all the colours around you from just red, yellow and blue. These three colours are called the primary colours.

9

Colours and patterns

You have now learnt to mix many different colours.

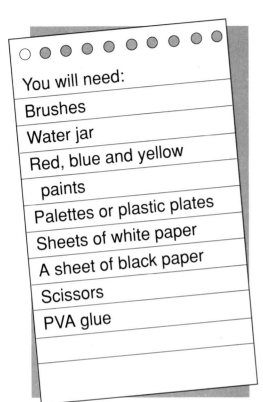

You will need:

Brushes

Water jar

Red, blue and yellow
 paints

Palettes or plastic plates

Sheets of white paper

A sheet of black paper

Scissors

PVA glue

Look again at the colours you have mixed. You are going to make a pattern using the oranges and purples.

- Paint stripes down the paper starting with yellowy orange.
- Add a tiny bit more red to your palette and paint the next stripe. Do not leave any paper showing between the stripes. When you run out of oranges, start on the purples.

When the paint is dry, turn the paper on its side.

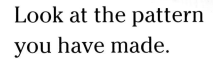

Look at the pattern you have made.

You can make a different pattern using another striped painting. Cut it into lots of different sized triangles and other shapes. Paste the shapes on to black paper to make a pattern.

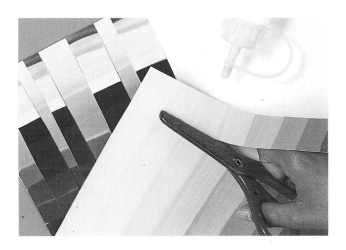

Cut a thin strip across the stripes and paste it on to another sheet of paper.
Now cut a wide strip, turn it the other way up and paste it on to the paper next to the first one. Paste on a third strip the right way up and so on until you have cut out and pasted all the strips.

Try making other patterns with some of the other colours.

Shapes and colours

Look at this painting – it is bigger than you are! It was painted in 1957 by an American artist called Mark Rothko.

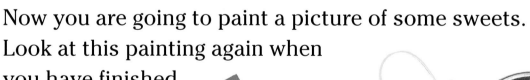

You will need:

A roll of frieze paper or wallpaper

Paper

Paints, including black

Palettes or plastic plates

Water jar

Liquorice allsorts

Glue

Scissors

Now you are going to paint a picture of some sweets. Look at this painting again when you have finished.

Put one of the sweets on the table in front of you.
- Mix your paints to the same colour as the sweet.
Paint the shape of the sweet. Make it big. Try not to go over the edges of your sweet shape.

Choose a different sweet. Do the same thing again. Carry on until you have painted all the shapes and colours.

If some of the sweets are striped, paint the stripes.

When you have finished, cut out your paintings and glue them to the large sheet of paper. Then put your paintings in a row on the wall.

Hot and cold colours

Some colours are known as 'hot' colours and some are known as 'cold' colours. Artists sometimes use these different colours to show how they are feeling when they paint. What colours do you think are hot? Think of a fire. What colour is it? Now think of the cold sea. What colours would you use to paint it?

You will need:

Paper

Brushes

Water jar

Paints

Palettes or plastic plates

Look at this painting *Dance Hall Scene* by Christopher Nevinson, an Englishman who lived about fifty years ago. Has he used hot or cold colours? Or both? Do you think it is a happy picture?

14

Paint a picture using hot or cold colours. Hot colours are reds, oranges and yellows. Cold colours are blues, purples and greens.

Think of a picture you would like to paint. It could be a cold snow scene, a stormy sea, or a rainy day. You could paint the hot sun, the desert or a fire with tall flames.

- Mix your colours carefully.
- Paint your background first. Paint the rest of your picture when the background is dry.

Try to mix lots of shades for your hot or cold colour painting.

Next time try different ideas and colours.

15

Textures

You can make your paintings look and feel different by adding textures.

You will need:
Powder paints
PVA glue
Old plastic bowls
Big brushes
Water jar
Stiff paper or card
A piece of bark
Sand

Texture is how things feel and look. It can be soft like velvet, bumpy like the bark of a tree, or spiky like a hedgehog or porcupine. What other textures can you think of?

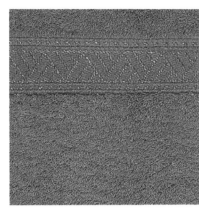

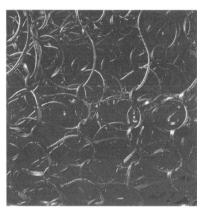

Mix paint, glue and a little water to make very thick paint.
Spread it on to the paper with a wide brush. If you carefully lift your brush at the end of each stroke you can make peaks of paint.

Use the end of the wooden handle to make different lines in the paint.

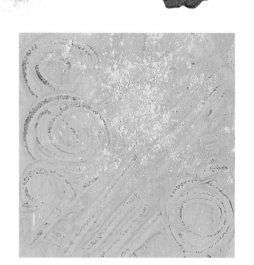

Try sprinkling tiny amounts of powder paint on to the painting.

Experiment with different amounts of paint, glue and water to make different thicknesses of paint.

Look at some wood bark. Try to make the same textures in your painting. Think of some other textures you could paint.

Take some sand and add it to your paint mixture. Paint textures with the sandy paint. Try just powder paint, sand and water.

Experiment with different ingredients and notice the different effects.

WARNING! Wash out your bowls and brushes as soon as you have finished painting or the glue will make them set hard!

Painting with texture

Look at this painting. It is called *Sunflowers*, by Vincent Van Gogh. He lived in Holland about 100 years ago. Look at the colours he has used.

Now look at the small picture. This is a close-up of part of *Sunflowers*. See how the artist has used thick paint to create the feel of the petals and add texture to his painting.

You can use thick paint to add texture to your paintings.

Look at *Sunflowers* again.

Put your vase of flowers on the table where you are drawing.

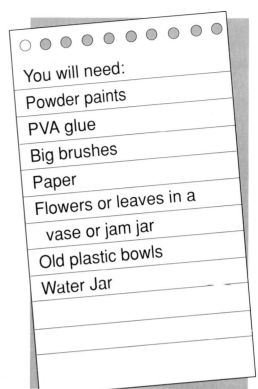

- Mix up your colours using powder paints and PVA glue.
  Paint the background to your picture first.
- Paint the flowers in the vase.
- Look carefully at their shapes and colours. Try to paint the same textures you see on the leaves and petals. Use the wooden end of your brush as well as the bristle end.

19

Painting animals

You can use texture to create animals with fur or feathers.

You will need:
Powder paints
Brushes
Card
Pencils
PVA glue
Old plastic bowls
Water jar
Sawdust
Earth

Draw a picture in pencil of your family pet or an animal you like. Sit as near to it as possible so that you can see what its fur or feathers are really like, or look at a large photograph. Look at the different colours.

Mix the glue and powder paints to make up the colours you want.

Divide the gluey paint into two sets of mixing bowls.

Add earth to one half and sawdust to the other. If it is too thick add water. Try them both on some card. Which works the best?

Now you are ready to paint your picture.

- Look at the animal's fur, hair or feathers.
- Paint your picture with the earth or sawdust mixture.
- Spread the mixture thinly on to the card.
- Think about the animal's coat. What lines and marks can you make to look like fur?
- Use the wooden end of your brush as before.
- Try using a nail, an old fork, or a comb to make different lines.

Finish your painting and cut it out.

Wax resist

Wax is waterproof so paint runs off it. You can use wax in your paintings.

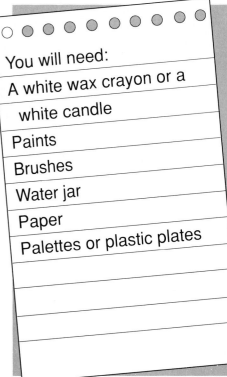

You will need:

A white wax crayon or a
  white candle
Paints
Brushes
Water jar
Paper
Palettes or plastic plates

- Draw some lines with the wax crayon.
- Mix some thin paint and brush it carefully over your drawing.

You can still see the lines you drew with the wax. This is called wax resist.

Make some different marks and try again.

Now you are ready to make a picture.

Draw it with the crayon. You can draw it lightly with a pencil and go over it if you find it hard to see your drawing in wax. Mix thin paint and go over your picture. Don't make the paper too wet.

Next time use lots of different coloured wax crayons. Draw a different picture or make a pattern and paint over it.

Painting with dots

Look closely at this painting. How do you think it has been painted? Can you see all the little dots? Painting with dots is called Pointillism.

Georges Seurat, a Frenchman who died about a hundred years ago, was one of the first people to paint this way. This painting by him is called *A Sunday Afternoon at the Grande Jatte*.

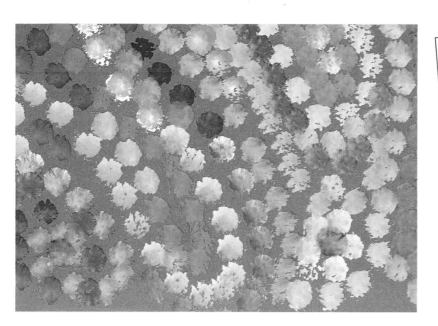

You will need:

Paints

Water jar

Paper

Stiff brushes

Palettes or plastic plates

You can paint with dots, too.

- Mix different colours. You should practise painting with dots first. Use the tip of the bristles to make dots of colour. Dab the brush up and down.
  You could use your finger too!
- Draw some wavy lines and paint in between them with dots. Keep the dots close together. Fill the whole page.

Paint a picture of sky and trees.

- Mix lots of blues. Paint dots close together to make the sky.
  Now mix lots of greens. Paint the trees.

Look at your picture close to and from across the room. Does it look different?

Through the window

Lots of artists have made paintings looking in or out of windows. You can make a painting looking through a window too.

Eric Ravilious was an English artist who lived in the first half of this century. His painting, *Train Landscape*, shows a view from a train window.

Edward Hopper, an American artist, lived about thirty years ago. This painting by him is called *Chop Suey*.

You have learned to mix colours and to paint in different ways. Which way did you like best? Choose your favourite for your next painting about windows.

Will your painting be from the inside looking out, or from the outside looking in? You could paint the view from your window, or think of a different view.

Here are some ideas. Imagine looking out of a submarine, castle or train, or looking into a spaceship. Can you think of any other scenes?

Think about different window shapes such as circles, squares and ovals.

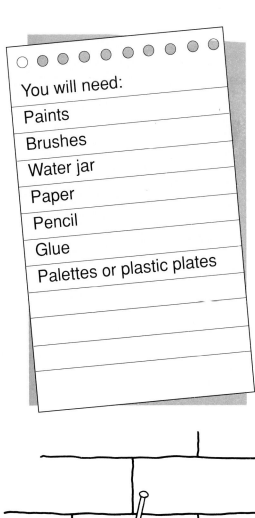

You will need:

Paints

Brushes

Water jar

Paper

Pencil

Glue

Palettes or plastic plates

Now paint your picture.

- Mix your colours carefully.
- Paint the background first.
- Remember the window frame!

When you have finished, hang your painting on the wall like a window.

Portraits

Look at this painting by Modigliani, an Italian artist who died in 1920. It is a portrait of Jeanne Hèbuterne. If you paint a picture of yourself it is called a self-portrait. Sometimes people in portraits are smiling; sometimes there are other things in the picture, such as their home or a family pet. They may be reading a book, or wearing special clothes which might give us a clue about who they are. What will you put in your picture?

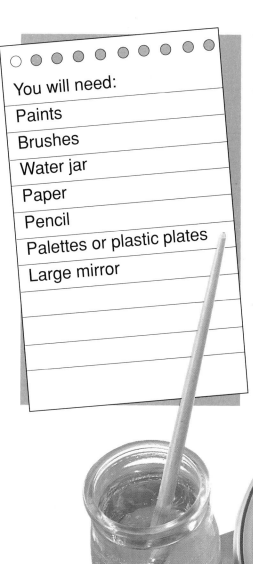

You will need:

Paints

Brushes

Water jar

Paper

Pencil

Palettes or plastic plates

Large mirror

Sit in front of a mirror and look closely at yourself. Look at the shape of your face, and your nose. What colour are your eyes? Are you smiling?
Practise drawing yourself once or twice.

Now you are ready to paint a self-portrait.

Mix your colours carefully.
Paint the outline of your head first.
Think about what else might be in your painting.
Paint these in the background.
Keep looking in the mirror and back at your painting until you have finished your portrait.

Next time paint a different picture of yourself.

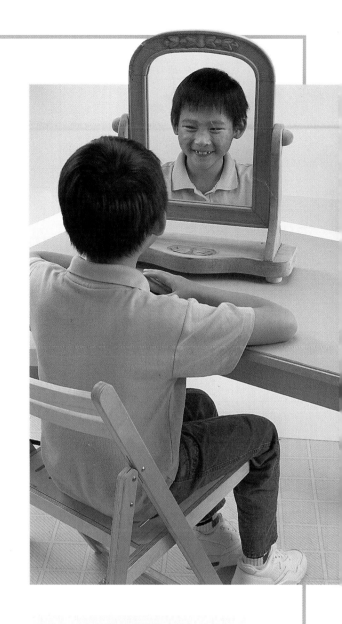

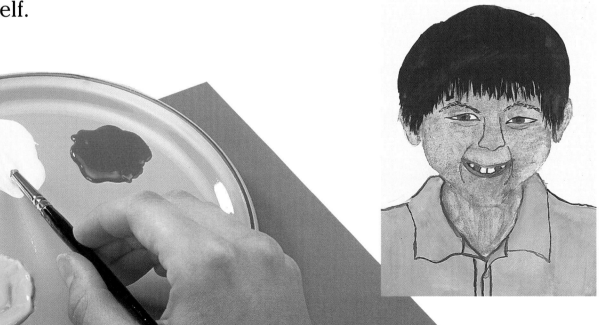

Notes for parents/teachers

FIRST ARTS & CRAFTS: PAINTING introduces the child to different techniques in painting. Inventiveness and experimentation are to be encouraged at all times. Where possible try to find contrasting examples to back up work in any media. Encourage discussion of this work and compare it. Get the children used to talking about their own work too. Art galleries and craft workshops will enable children to see first hand art in the making as well as the finished result. Showing children paintings from a book is of great value, but there is nothing quite like looking at the real thing – which may turn out to be bigger than they are!

Looking at colours 4 - 5
Encourage children to discuss the colours around them. Make as big a collection of examples of colours as you can find, and that children can add to. Group some colours together, mix others. Collect different photographs and magazine illustrations of skies and seas, and compare them. Compare paintings from different periods where strong colour has been used to paint sky or landscape.

Brushes and techniques 6 - 7
Make available as many different types of brush as possible including decorators' paintbrushes. Combine some techniques, e.g. after sponging try spatter painting on top. The bristles of the paintbrushes can be pulled back and released, as well as using the toothbrush and comb technique, but it can be messy. Screen the area with newsprint. Older children could use a diffuser. Encourage children to mix colours and experiment with them while trying out the techniques. Compare examples of water-colour and oil paintings. See how varied brushwork, paint and style create different effects.

Colour mixing 8 - 9
As general experimenting with mixing colour has been tried in the previous section, this approach is more controlled. Emphasize how small an amount of different colour paint can alter an existing colour. Demonstrate, then let them try before starting a complete exercise. Paint should be the consistency of thin cream. Do not let the paper swim with water. In class you could have a competition to make the longest line of different shades and colours. Select something from the children's display of coloured objects. Can they mix the colour? Do not use black or white.

Colours and patterns 10 - 11
The appearance of the colour strips will vary tremendously according to the width of the brush used and on whether you paint the paper lengthways or widthways. Get the children to experiment with these different ways. Older children could weave strips: it is easier if the vertical sections are held in place by taping the tops to a backing sheet which can be cut away afterwards. Results will also vary according to whether just two or three colour ranges are mixed or whether more colours are introduced. Experiment. Lay strips on to different coloured backgrounds and 'explode' the painting by placing strips in ever-increasing distances apart. When triangular and random shapes have been cut and stuck down, ask the children to look at the negative space, i.e. the shape and pattern made between the solid shapes.

Shapes and colours 12 - 13
Encourage children to paint straight on to the paper and not to draw first. Liquorice allsorts are particularly good because they introduce children to shape and form, looking at circles and squares as well as varied colours. The pink will be more difficult to achieve if you are using a 'yellow' red such as vermilion. Try a 'blue' red such as crimson. Mixing brown may prove difficult as it involves all three primary colours. Join several sheets of paper together and ask each child to paint a really large sweet. Make a wall of sweets. Show the children more examples of Rothko's work, similar to the one already shown. A recommended book is *Mark Rothko: Subjects in Abstraction* by Anne C. Chave.

Hot and cold colours 14 - 15
Gather more examples of artists' work. Possibilities include Paul Nash's *We are making a New World*, any Klimt portraits with bright colours, David Bomberg's *The Red Hat* and Edvard Munch's *The Cry*. Use Nash's work, Turner's *Snowstorm at Sea* and *Steamboat off a Harbour's Mouth,* Monet's series of paintings of haystacks and Rouen Cathedral plus other paintings showing bright sunny days, or those depicting fire or flames, snow or rain. Encourage the children to compare them and say which pictures use hot colours and which cold. Do any make the children feel happy, or sad and gloomy? Ask them to say why.

Textures 16 - 17
As mentioned in the text, the media mixtures used in the next three sections will set if left. PVA mixed in water and paint will not set for a while so there is plenty of time to complete the exercise as long as everything is then washed. The glue is water soluble so brushes can be washed in the sink. It is important to think about surface texture while working on this

section. Collect examples of texture. Pass them around. Get the children to feel each example with their eyes closed, and describe the feel of the texture, then open their eyes and describe how it looks. Encourage children to experiment with their own ideas to create texture. Squares and rectangles could be cut out to make a panel in relief. Hang it on the wall. Parts of it could be sponged and spattered.

Painting with texture 18 - 19

The flowers should be at eye level. Get the child to look very closely at them and to keep looking back at them all the time. Collect other examples of Van Gogh's work to look at when this section has been completed, e.g. *Portrait of the Artist* and *Wheatfield with Cypresses*. Look at the texture and movement created by the contour lines which often follow and emphasize shapes. Get the children to describe what they see. An extension of this work is to paint a picture from imagination, e.g. of the sun. Use contour lines around it to emphasize movement in the sky. Invent other marks in the paint to show texture.

Painting animals 20 - 21

Collect photographs and paintings of animals. Kaffe Fassett's book *Glorious Inspiration* has some good examples of animals painted by many artists. Encourage the children to look at as many living animals as they can, looking at their coats, touching them if possible and describing how they feel and look. Get the children to: sketch animals with big charcoal sticks, graphite or chalks; draw silhouettes of animals and think about outline shape; fill in with black paint or draw on black paper and cut out; think about what will make the best marks for the animal's coat. In class make a pets' corner. Put a frieze on the wall with branches, leaves and grass. Cut out animal and bird paintings, drawings and silhouettes, and assemble them on the frieze. For other work children could paint an animal from a story or make up an imaginary animal and give it a name.

Wax resist 22 - 23

Henry Moore's *Shelter* drawings are wonderful examples of wax resist, as are some of his other works. The paint needs to be thin like a wash, but able to cover. Do not let the painting get saturated. Children should paint a wash, as in *Brushes and techniques* p6 - 7, but should not over paint or the wax will eventually come off. Encourage children to make lots of different marks with the crayon e.g. dots, running lines, zig zags, hatching and cross-hatching. Further work could be a picture of a rainy or snowy day using just black or grey paint. Alternatively the children could make large holiday postcards with lots of sun, clouds and sea. Both these subjects link in with earlier work in the book. With supervision candle wax could be melted down in a washed and dried tin-can standing in a saucepan of hot water. Drip and trail wax onto card. Look at the different effects when painted over. Batik is the technique of painting or dripping wax on to fabric, which is then dyed and, when dry, ironed between sheets of brown paper to melt and remove the wax. It must only be done under supervision. You can buy special batik wax and tools.

Painting with dots 24 - 25

Other paintings to refer to are works by Seurat and Signac. An extension of this work is to look at light and dark, e.g. where shadows and highlights are. Get each child to paint another scene of trees with dots of colour. They should look out of the window at a tree if possible, but if not they can use a photograph. Get them to use yellow dots close together to show where the tree is lightest, and dark blues and purples to show shadows. They can compare it to their first tree picture.

Through the window 26 - 27

Encourage children to try the different techniques they have been introduced to in this book. Collect photographs. Discuss other places where you find different window shapes and scenes. Introduce them to ideas linked with the past – temples, castles and dungeons, for instance, and with scenes in other countries. Discuss the chosen window shape, the viewpoint, and the content of the view. It could be a painting of their own bedroom or a view from another room in the house or classroom. An extension of this work could be to make a three dimensional scene. Get the children to paint the background separately, then make and paint, using paint and PVA glue, a window frame. Stick this on to the background. Paint and cut out items for the foreground and glue those on last of all, making three layers. Windows have been a recurring theme for artists throughout history, and they will feature again in this series too! An invaluable help for the windows theme, and indeed many other themes, is a series of postcard packs each containing twenty-four examples of artists' work (obtainable from Goodwill Art Packs - 071 602 6465).

Portraits 28 - 29

For the self-portrait children should be encouraged to sit in front of a large mirror looking back at themselves as they paint. Extension work, especially in a classroom situation, would be to concentrate on facial expression. Take photographs to refer to later. This work could then lead on to portraits of other children or a member of the family. Choose contrasting examples of artists' work in terms of technique, period and subject matter e.g. Rembrandt, Gwen John and David Hockney, to show the children. The National Portrait Gallery in London (071 306 0055) offers extensive information, postcard packs and guided tours. For school parties there are workshops available and an advisory specialist to help with the tour of the gallery.

Further information

Glossary

Ingredients Different things that are put together to make something else.
Pattern Shapes and colours that are repeated.
Pointillism Painting with dots.
Portrait A picture of a person or animal.
Primary colours Red, blue and yellow. Nearly all other colours are made from these.

PVA glue Water based glue.
Self-portrait A picture of oneself.
Techniques In this book, the different ways of painting.
Texture The feel or look of a surface.
Wash A thin coating of watery colour over the paper.
Wax resist Using wax to keep areas free of paint.

Index

Acknowledgements

The publishers wish to thank the following for the use of photographs:
City of Aberdeen Art Gallery and Museums Collections for Eric Ravilious' *Train Landscape*;
Visual Arts Library for Van Gogh's *Sunflowers* (page 18 and cover), Claude Monet's *Impression, Sunrise*, Georges Seurat's *A Sunday Afternoon at the Grande Jatte* and Amedeo Modigliani's *Jeanne Hèbuterne*;
© 1993 Kate Rothko - Prizel and Christopher Rothko/ARS New York for Mark Rothko's *Untitled 1957*;
The Hopper Collections, Witney Museum of American Art for Edward Hopper's *Chop Suey*;
The Tate Gallery, London for Christopher Nevinson's *Dance Hall Scene* and
The Turner Collection, The Tate Gallery, London for J.M.W. Turner's *Tours: Sunset*.

The publishers also wish to thank our models – Alana, Chloe, Manlai and Reechal, and our young artists Rebecca and Sue.